Photography Art

original images

Joseph Fleming

Joseph Fleming

Custom Quality Original Artwork

Decades of being around accomplished talent producing absolutely phenomenal quality work has taught that we are capable of greatness. It is possible to meet our destiny and become it. Experiencing excellence done with such apparent ease and humble selfless gratification is the motivation for this photography. Most important was having the freedom

Being colorblind gives an advantage when composing black & white… less confusion. This special collection selected from thousands of captures. All images were framed in the camera and presented without edits, genuine as seen through the lens. RAW conversion applied by proprietary panchromatic process.

Limited edition prints available from source files. Contact for custom work.

info@ BEACHNOISE.com

0125

0351

0354

0503

0531

0705

0780

0826

0920

0938

1085

1088

1581

1608

1784

1976

2068

2180

2397

2467

2495

2631

2929

2962

3147

3151

3359

3656

3720

3799

3916

3937

3943

4035

4070

4099

4193

4265

4533

4560

4879

5492

5541

5705

5708

5750

5784

5811

5844

5846

6014

6095

6176

6946

7148

7182

7339

7656

7693

7783

7843

7939

8173

8345

8407

8470

8471

8766

8889

9024

9297

9353

9430

9970

9975

9980

9992

9993

9998

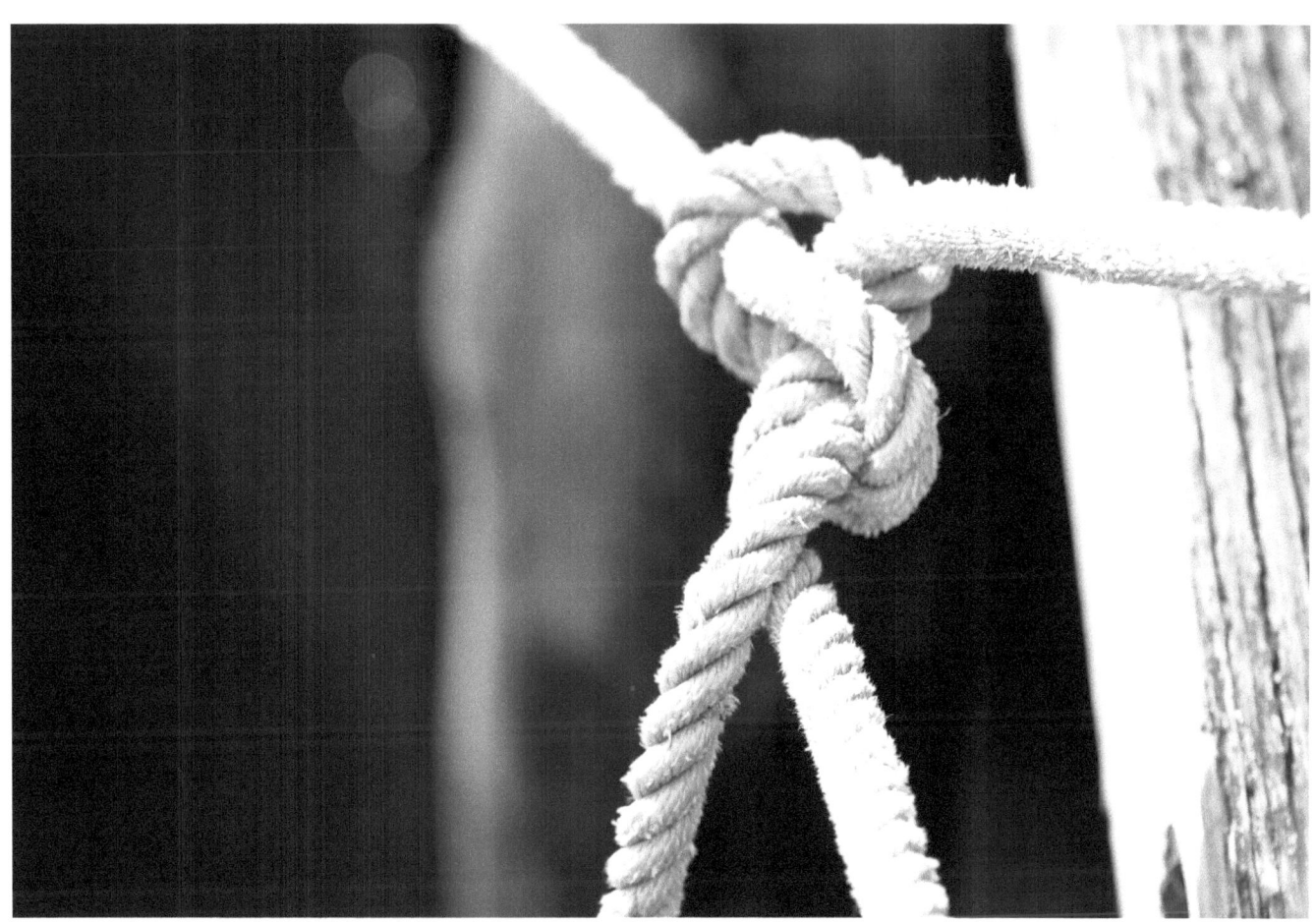

10003

www.ingramcontent.com/pod-product-compliance
Lightning Source LLC
Chambersburg PA
CBHW050735180526
45159CB00003B/1242

9 781507 535226